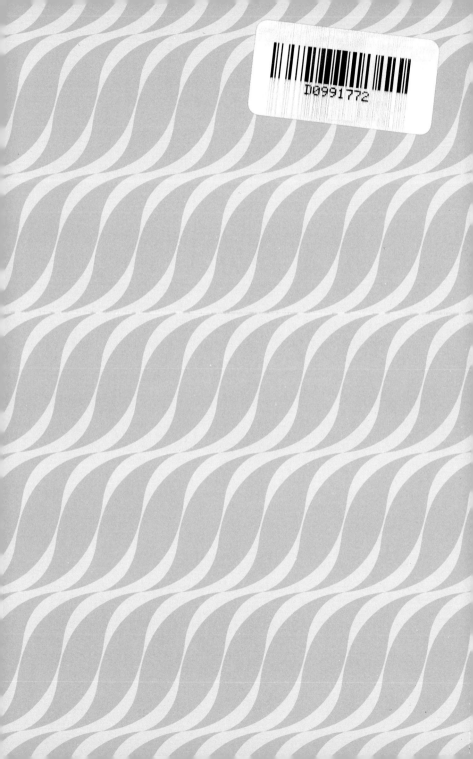

THE NEW PLANT LIBRARY

GRASSES

THE NEW PLANT LIBRARY

GRASSES

JO CHATTERTON

Consultant: Trevor Scott

southwater

This edition is published by Southwater

Distributed in the UK by the Manning Partnership
251–253 London Road East
Batheaston, Bath BA1 7RL
tel. 01225 852 727; fax 01225 852 852

Published in the USA by Anness Publishing Inc.
27 West 20th Street, Suite 504
New York NY 10011
fax 212 807 6813

Distributed in Canada by General Publishing
895 Don Mills Road, 400–402 Park Centre
Toronto, Ontario M3C 1W3
tel. 416 445 3333; fax 416 445 5991

Distributed in Australia by Sandstone Publishing
Unit 1, 360 Norton Street
Leichhardt, New South Wales 2040
tel. 02 9560 7888; fax 02 9560 7488

Southwater is an imprint of Anness Publishing Limited
Hermes House, 88–89 Blackfriars Road, London SE1 8HA
tel. 020 7401 2077; fax 020 7633 9499
© Anness Publishing Limited 1998, 2001

Publisher: Joanna Lorenz
Senior Editor: Cathy Marriott
Designer: Michael Morey
Photographer: Jonathan Buckley
Production Controller: Joanna King

Previously published in a larger format

1 3 5 7 9 10 8 6 4 2

■ HALF TITLE PAGE
Miscanthus group.

■ FRONTISPIECE
Sales area at Wisley
Gardens.

■ TITLE PAGE
Hakonechloa macra
'Alboaurea'.

■ LEFT
Typha latifolia.

■ OPPOSITE LEFT
*Pennisetum
alopecuroides.*

■ OPPOSITE RIGHT
Miscanthus sinensis
'Malepartus'.

Contents

Introduction

*I*n this book the term grasses includes the true grasses and bamboos and the unrelated grass-like sedges. These plant families (Gramineae or Poaceae in the case of grasses and bamboos, and Cyperaceae of sedges) are now becoming increasingly popular with gardeners as their striking potential is gradually being realized.

Whatever the climate, position, soil condition or size of space available there is a grass that will be suitable, each with its own attraction, able to contribute to the garden in a unique way. There are wonderful grasses that can provide height and shelter, spiky accents, feathery waves, and neat, low-growing clumps. Even better, many grasses retain their delightful structure through the winter months giving added texture to the garden skeleton.

■ RIGHT
A fine collection of grasses with mixed planting creates a variety of form and texture.

The history of grasses

The cultivation of grasses is as old as gardening itself. The grass family produces the world's cereal crops and is an essential element of the human and farmed animal food supply.

Although each region of the world has its own native grasses, it is only relatively recently that garden cultivars have been introduced for their beauty of form and structure. The popular *Cortaderia selloana* (Pampas grass) was introduced into Europe from South America in the mid-19th century. The Irish gardener and writer William Robinson (1838–1935) favoured the natural appearance of uncut grass waving in the wind over neatly trimmed lawns. In the 20th century, garden grasses have been used to create a variety of effects. Gertrude Jekyll liked to include lyme grass (*Leymus arenarius*) in her colourful flower borders for its blue foliage and vertical accent. She also used *Miscanthus sinensis* in other planting schemes for its bold form amongst other perennials. But in the second half of the century the emphasis has been on more natural landscapes in Europe and North America. The contemporary North American landscape architect, Wolfgang Oehme, has helped establish such a growing trend. So too did the German plantsman Karl Foerster (1874–1970), who did much to introduce the use of new varieties of grass. The strikingly upright *Calamagrostis* x *acutiflora* 'Karl Foerster' is named after him.

Natural landscaping makes use of grasses and perennials planted in bold groups, or intermingled to create a meadow-like effect. Interest after the summer flowering season is provided by skeletal shapes and interesting seed heads. These gardens are designed to be low maintenance and, because mainly native plants are used, they are well adapted to their environment. Such planting schemes are now being increasingly used in parks and public spaces as a refreshing change from the more traditional, artificial look.

■ OPPOSITE
Stipa tenuissima in a naturalistic planting,
with late perennials and architectural
seed heads.

■ LEFT
Bamboo is often
used as hedging in
Asia. Here the
idea has been
transposed to a
Western style
gravel garden.

■ BELOW LEFT
Bamboos were
introduced to the
West in the late 19th
century. Here the
height and fine
foliage of *Phyllo-
stachys viridi-
glaucescens* contrast
beautifully with the
large leaves of
Gunnera manicata
and the feathery
fringe of *Equisetum*.

Oriental influences

In south and south-east Asia bamboos
are an integral part of the landscape,
both natural and cultivated,
ornamental and utilitarian. For
centuries bamboo has been grown as
a food, building material, and for
making paper. Bamboo was known
to botanists in Europe as early as the
late 18th century, but it was not
until the 19th century that it was
grown in Britain and North America.
Today it is ubiquitous in gardens, if
only in the form of cane plant
supports. The general introduction
of bamboo in Britain is largely due to
A.B. Freeman-Mitford (1837–1916)

who became Lord Redesdale. In
the 1890s he sent many varieties of
bamboo to Britain from Japan, and
in 1896 published *The Bamboo
Garden*, which helped increase the
plant's popularity.

In the 19th century Japanese art
and culture became popular in the
West, and as trade links opened
many of the beauties of Japanese
gardening were introduced. This
style was particularly influential in
Europe and Britain as the antidote
to the garish Victorian bedding
schemes which were then prevalent,

and which are still cherished by
many who are responsible for
planting British and European parks.
The oriental style encompassed
refined simplicity and a contemp-
lative garden philosophy with its
carefully placed components of rock,
water and plant. Grasses such as
Miscanthus sinensis and *Hakonechloa
macra*, and Japanese bamboos such
as *Pleioblastus*, *Sasa* and *Shibataea*,
were planted for their graceful effect
and symbolism. Bamboos have
also been cultivated in China and
Japan as bonsai.

Grasses as garden plants

The wide diversity of grasses available ensures that there is usually at least one type for every garden situation. They look well when grouped together, or used as single specimens. Often grasses work particularly well when associated with other plants. Their airy form and movement contrasts effectively with larger leaved plants, and their vertical accent lifts and lightens dense groupings.

Grasses for shade

In shady areas the brightly variegated foliage of *Carex hachijoensis* 'Evergold' will shine out all the year round. Other shade-tolerant variegated grasses include *Molinia caerulea* ssp.

■ LEFT
An attractive waterside planting including *Carex elata* 'Aurea' and *Miscanthus sinensis* 'Zebrinus'.

GRASSES FOR AUTUMN COLOUR

Chasmanthium latifolium

Hakonechloa macra 'Alboaurea'

Imperata cylindrica 'Rubra'

Miscanthus sinensis var. *purpurascens*

Molinia caerulea ssp. *caerulea* 'Variegata'

Pennisetum alopecuroides

Phalaris arundinacea 'Tricolor'

Stipa arundinacea

caerulea 'Variegata', *Hakonechloa macra* 'Alboaurea' and 'Aureola' and *Phalaris arundinacea* var. *picta* 'Picta'. They complement other shade-loving plants such as hostas, ferns and hydrangeas.

Areas of dry shade are difficult to plant successfully but *Stipa arundinacea* copes with these inhospitable conditions, and makes an attractive combination planted with a skirt of *Bergenia cordifolia* for winter interest. Shady woodland areas can be carpeted with the golden foliage of *Milium effusum* 'Aureum', or with varieties of *Deschampsia cespitosa*, which have elegant flower spikes that catch the light beautifully in a woodland setting.

Grasses for planting by water

Many grasses also look attractive planted by water. The striking *Cortaderia selloana* (Pampas grass), and taller varieties such as *Miscanthus*, are impressive when planted in large clumps beside a lake or large pond. Their upright structure provides a contrasting accent against the horizontal plane of the water. Many bamboos also have this effect, and their lush foliage can give an almost tropical feel to a marginal planting scheme. Some grasses such as *Glyceria maxima, Carex elata* 'Aurea' and *Spartina pectinata* are happy to be treated as marginals, and appreciate the damp conditions by the water's edge. They offset other marginals with bold foliage such as *Lysichiton americanus* and the enormous leaves of *Gunnera manicata.*

■ ABOVE
A collection of grasses in containers makes a versatile display for a small garden, terrace or balcony.

■ BELOW
A maze created out of *Oryzopsis lessoniana* is a striking, unusual use of this grass. Low-growing grasses can also be used in parterres.

■ LEFT
An excellent example of how grasses add height, texture and movement to a mixed border.

Grasses for sunny positions

Many blue and silvery leaved grasses are suitable for growing in dry, sunny gardens. *Helictotrichon sempervirens*, varieties of *Festuca glauca, Poa labillardieri* and *Leymus arenarius* all have attractive blue-grey foliage and thrive in full sun. They can be used in a cool colour scheme of blues, greys and whites by combining them with other sun lovers such as *Stachys byzantina, Salvia officinalis, Iris pallida*, the white rose 'Iceberg' and blue agapanthus. Alternatively, in a

A more invasive plant for naturalizing in damp conditions is the bulrush *Typha latifolia*. Since it can spread rapidly its roots should be contained in smaller gardens to prevent it from swamping less vigorous plants. *Scirpoides holo-* *schoenus* and the soft rush *Juncus effusus* are also useful marginal plants for the water's edge. For the conservatory there is *Cyperus involucratus* and *C. papyrus* which need damp conditions; they can even be planted in shallow water.

■ LEFT
For a summer bedding display use this brightly variegated grass which contrasts strikingly with the dark foliage of *Perilla frutescens* var. *crispa*.

■ OPPOSITE
The texture and movement provided by this grass contrasts well with the more solid architectural planting behind.

■ RIGHT
Contrasting silvery-blue foliage for a sunny garden with *Festuca glauca, Convolvulus cneorum* and variegated iris.

scheme using hotter colours, try grasses that fade to pale gold in late summer such as *Stipa calamagrostis, Stipa tenuissima* and *Calamagrostis x acutiflora* 'Karl Foerster'. They create a vibrant scene when planted with later flowering perennials such as *Rudbeckia, Helenium* and *Crocosmia.* This type of planting has been used to great effect in large-scale schemes in North America to make a prairie-like landscape. To create an unusual arena for a display of drought-tolerant grasses such as *Stipa tenuissima* and *Stipa gigantea,* as well as the sun-lovers mentioned above, try a dry gravel garden.

Grasses for small gardens

Low-growing and clump-forming grasses are suitable for growing in small gardens. Where space is limited, evergreens such as *Carex hachijoensis* 'Evergold' and *Festuca glauca* varieties are particularly useful for their continuing winter presence. Taller grasses such as *Miscanthus sinensis* varieties and *Calamagrostis x acutiflora* 'Karl Foerster' can also be incorporated in smaller gardens as they provide a useful vertical accent, and are non-invasive. Many bamboos are unsuitable for small gardens because of their large size and tendency to spread. However, smaller varieties

plant pot, whereas the upright form of *Imperata cylindrica* 'Rubra' looks best in a shallower container. One of the advantages of planting grasses in containers is that they can be moved around. Try placing them so that they are backlit by the evening or early morning light. Since grasses generally cope well with exposed situations they can be grown on balconies where other plants may fail. Remember to water containers regularly, especially where the wind dries out the soil.

Other uses for grasses

Grasses can also extend the period of interest in the garden as many look their best in late summer when other garden plants are past their peak flowering time. *Miscanthus* varieties not only flower in late summer and autumn, but the flowering stems continue to stand upright through the winter months when the foliage has died back. *Pennisetum alopecuroides* turns a striking orange-red in autumn to complement the tawny tints of other autumn foliage, and if left to stand in winter, many seed heads have a delicate skeletal appearance when covered by frost. For spring interest *Milium effusum*

such as *Pleioblastus auricomus* with yellow variegated leaves, *P. variegatus* with white variegated leaves, and the compact *Shibataea kumasasa* take up relatively little space.

The light, airy forms of grasses provide a wonderful contrast with solid structures such as walls, masonry and paving. Courtyard gardens, terraces and balconies are ideal for growing grasses in containers. There

are many varieties that can be grown in this way. Varying the size and shape of the container will give additional interest to a grouping. For example, a bamboo such as *Phyllostachys nigra* works well in a large container surrounded by smaller pots, or even standing alone as a specimen. The rounded bun-shape of *Hakonechloa macra* 'Alboaurea' suits the shape of an ordinary terracotta

from being divided when they become overcrowded. Herbaceous types can be cut back in spring, and then left for the rest of the year. Evergreen grasses may need to be groomed in spring to remove any dead foliage, but otherwise their needs are few. Another benefit is that grasses are generally free from pests and diseases.

'Aureum' is a fresh greeny-yellow early in the season. It grows best in dappled shade, as does another early performer, *Carex pendula*. This has attractive hanging flower spikes in spring and early summer.

Larger grasses and bamboos can be used for hedging and screening. Bamboos are generally evergreen and make effective permanent barriers. *Pleioblastus variegatus* makes an interesting low-growing screen with its brightly variegated foliage. For taller screens and hedges *Phyllostachys* cultivars are useful, as is an avenue of the evergreen *Cortaderia selloana* and its cultivars, which look particularly attractive in autumn and winter with their feathery plumes.

Apart from their wide versatility, grasses have the advantage of being low maintenance plants. As with most perennials, grasses benefit

■ ABOVE LEFT
Sasa veitchii and ferns make ideal companions for a shady area.

■ LEFT
The striking form of this pampas grass (*Cortaderia selloana* 'Albo-lineata') adds interest to the garden in autumn and winter.

Botany and classification

There are four families of grasses: Gramineae or Poaceae (true grasses and bamboos), Cyperaceae (sedges), Juncaceae (rushes) and Typhaceae (reedmaces). The largest of these is the Gramineae with many thousands of species. *Acorus gramineus* 'Variegatus', a member of the Araceae family, has been included in the plant catalogue because of its grass-like appearance. All the plants in these families are monocots, having only one primary leaf when grown from seed.

Stem structure

The stems, or culms, of the grass family are cylindrical and are usually hollow. Bamboos also have cylindrical stems, which are hollow except for *Chusquea* which has solid stems. Rushes and sedges have solid stems; those of rushes are cylindrical, and those of sedges triangular. The culms of bamboos and larger grasses have sheaths for protection. These become papery when mature, and eventually drop off to reveal the culms beneath. The colour of the culms can vary from black in *Phyllostachys nigra*, through shades of green to the muted yellow of *Phyllostachys*

aurea. The culms in most varieties of bamboo obtain their ultimate height and diameter in one growing season.

Leaf form

With grasses, the bases of the leaves form split sheaths around the stems, whereas in sedges and rushes the leaves form unbroken sheaths from which the stems emerge. The leaves of grasses and sedges have veins arranged in parallel lines. Leaves may be herbaceous and die back in winter, or they may be evergreen. The foliage of annual grasses is usually inconspicuous. In perennials there is a great variety of leaf colour and form

from the thin, blue spikes of *Festuca glauca* to the broad, flat leaves of *Arundo donax*. Bamboos are evergreen in their native climate, but some may lose their leaves in colder conditions. Their leaves are generally a narrow oval in shape (i.e. lanceolate, being shaped like a lance head), sometimes with variegation as in *Pleioblastus auricomus* and *P. variegatus*. Unlike grasses and sedges, bamboos have leaves with veins that are arranged like a mosaic (tessellated).

Flowers and reproduction

Grasses, sedges and rushes are all wind pollinated. Grasses have tiny flowers enclosed in pairs of bracts. A number of flowers together form a spikelet, and the spikelets together are the flower heads, which in some varieties are highly ornamental. The number of flowers and spikelets varies between grasses. Sedges have a similar arrangement, but generally the flower heads are less showy than those of true grasses. The flowers of grasses and rushes are usually bisexual and those of sedges unisexual, the flowers of both sexes appearing on the same plant. Annual grasses are best grown from seed, but it is rare for cultivated varieties of perennials to come true

■ BELOW
Stipa calamagrostis in early season.

■ LEFT
Stipa cala-magrostis in late season.

■ LEFT
Miscanthus sinensis 'Malepartus'.

■ LEFT
Pennisetum alopecuroides.

■ LEFT
The bamboo *Himalayacalamus falconeri* flowers and appears to degenerate. New growth should then emerge from the base.

production of flowers. Most plants recover eventually. Plants are classified botanically by studying their reproductive parts. Because of the rarity of bamboo flowers, establishing the identity of a genus has been difficult, which has led to many changes in nomenclature, especially in the genus *Arundinaria* which now has very few species after reclassification.

Root systems

Grasses have fibrous roots. Many also have creeping underground stems called rhizomes from which new growth emerges. Some plants such as *Glyceria maxima* and *Leymus arenarius* can become invasive through the rapid spread of their rhizomes. Some grasses also spread by stolons (stems that run along the ground and set roots) leading to the emergence of new shoots. The rhizomes of bamboos are either running, with one or more main rhizomes making a line from which culms emerge, or clumping, with many bulbous rhizomes close together giving rise to culms. Generally, the clumping types of bamboo are hardy only in their native tropical climates, whereas running bamboos can be grown successfully in colder regions and are more invasive.

from seed, and they are best propagated by division. The *Typha* genus (Bulrush, Reedmace or Cat's tail) have compact cylinders of brown velvety flowers along the stem. Both male and female flowers are borne on the same stem. Bamboos have inconspicuous flowers that appear infrequently and erratically. Often the plant appears to die back when it flowers as the plant concentrates its energies and nutrients into the

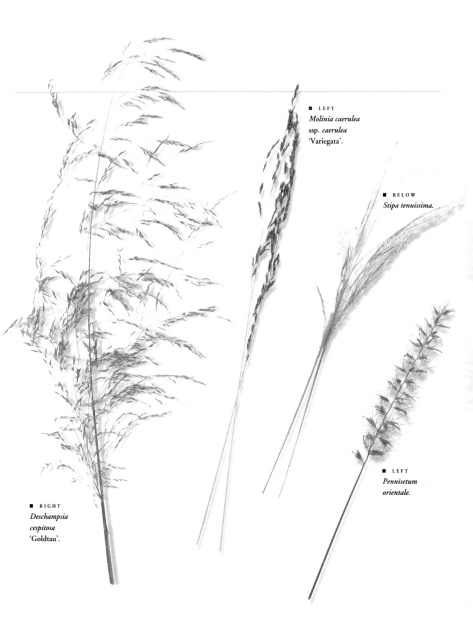

■ LEFT
Molinia caerulea
ssp. *caerulea*
'Variegata'.

■ BELOW
Stipa tenuissima.

■ LEFT
Pennisetum
orientale.

■ RIGHT
Deschampsia
cespitosa
'Goldtau'.

The following section provides
details of a selection of grasses
that have been grouped into
three categories: small – up to
60cm (2ft), medium – 60cm–
1.2m (2–4ft) and large – over
1.2m (4ft). The measurements
are the approximate height when
the plant is mature but may
vary depending on cultivation,
situation and climate. Plants
that normally survive winter
temperatures of –15°C (5°F)
are listed as hardy but situation,
climate and soil type may affect
a plant's performance. All are
perennial except where noted.

Small grasses

■ ABOVE RIGHT
ACORUS GRAMINEUS
'VARIEGATUS'
───────────────────

This hardy plant from eastern Asia is ideal
for a bog garden, or growing in a shallow
pond. The variegated green and cream,
striped, smooth foliage falls outwards
from the centre of the plant. Height
and spread to 30cm (1ft). It prefers full
sun and moist conditions. The variety
'Ogon' has yellowish-green and cream
variegated foliage.

■ RIGHT
BRIZA MINOR (LESSER
QUAKING GRASS)
───────────────────

A hardy annual grass from Europe and
Asia which is grown from seed. The
flowers resemble tiny pendants spread on a
branching flower head, and are useful for
dried flower arrangements. Height 60cm
(2ft), spread 30cm (1ft). It tolerates most
soil conditions, preferring a sunny
position. The perennial form, *B. media*
(Quaking grass), reaches 1m (3ft) high.

■ BELOW
CAREX CONICA 'SNOWLINE'

A cultivated variety of the species originating in south-east Asia.
This hardy neat sedge makes small clumps. Height and spread
30cm (1ft). It has dark green leaves strikingly edged with white,
and being evergreen provides an interesting front of border plant
throughout the year. It is suitable for growing in containers, and
prefers a moisture-retentive soil in sun or partial shade.

■ ABOVE
CAREX ELATA 'AUREA', SYN. *C. STRICTA*
'AUREA' (BOWLES' GOLDEN SEDGE)

This hardy European variety was made popular by the British
plantsman E.A. Bowles (1865–1954). A herbaceous sedge with
slender arching foliage of greenish-gold. Height and spread to
60cm (2ft). It prefers moist soil, and grows well at the margins of
water. It also tolerates sun or partial shade and is suitable for
container planting, if kept well watered.

■ LEFT
CAREX 'FROSTED CURLS'

Of garden origin, this is a relative of *C. comans* which is a native of
New Zealand. It is a hardy low-growing sedge with pale green,
lustrous, narrow leaves that curl at the tips and tend to clump
together. Height and spread to 30cm (1ft). It prefers moist soil in a
sunny or partly shaded position.

■ ABOVE
CAREX TESTACEA

This hardy New Zealand sedge has pale olive-green leaves with bronze tints. Height and spread to 45cm (18in). It forms a rounded spreading mound of fine foliage. It requires a moisture-retentive soil and a sunny position. Being evergreen, its unusual colours make it an asset in the garden all year round. It is suitable for container planting.

■ ABOVE
CAREX HACHIJOENSIS 'EVERGOLD', SYN.
C. MORROWII 'EVERGOLD', *C. OSHIMENSIS*
'EVERGOLD'

A low-growing hardy sedge from Japan that forms a rounded clump. The foliage is evergreen and variegated, with a cream coloured central stripe and green margins. The flowers are inconspicuous. Height and spread to 30cm (1ft). It prefers moist soil, and a shady or semi-shady position. This is a particularly good plant for lightening the winter garden with its bright foliage, and is suitable for container planting.

■ RIGHT
CAREX MORROWII 'VARIEGATA'

A hardy, cultivated variety of the species from Japan. This sedge forms an evergreen, rounded clump of narrow foliage, radiating from the centre. Height and spread to 30cm (1ft). The leaves are variegated with white stripes against a dark green background. It prefers part shade or sun and a moisture-retentive soil. It is an attractive plant for the front of a shady border.

■ RIGHT
FESTUCA GLAUCA (BLUE FESCUE GRASS)

This European hardy grass makes a compact, spiky clump of fine, blue-grey leaves. Height and spread to 30cm (1ft). The flowers are borne in summer. It is evergreen and prefers a sunny position and well-drained soil. It is suitable for growing in containers.

■ BELOW LEFT
ELYMUS MAGELLANICUS

A hardy north Asian grass that has spiky leaves of steely blue-grey, making compact clumps. The pale flower spikes are borne in summer. It requires full sun and a well-drained soil. Height and spread to 45cm (18in). It is excellent in a container.

■ BELOW RIGHT
HAKONECHLOA MACRA 'ALBOAUREA'

This hardy Japanese herbaceous grass makes a rounded cushion of tapering foliage. The leaves are variegated with yellow and green stripes, turning russet in the autumn. Small flowers are borne in summer and early autumn. Height and spread to 45cm (18in). It prefers a moisture-retentive soil in shade or part shade, and is suitable for growing in containers. *H. macra* 'Aureola' is very similar.

■ LEFT

HORDEUM JUBATUM (FOXTAIL BARLEY, SQUIRREL-TAIL BARLEY)

This hardy annual grass from North America and north-east Asia has plumes of showy flowers in late summer and early autumn. It prefers full sun and a well-drained soil. Height 60cm (2ft), spread 30cm (1ft). The attractive flowers make it a useful plant for drying and flower arranging.

■ ABOVE

MELICA CILIATA

A hardy European, North African and south-west Asian grass, with mounds of grey-green foliage. Pale flower heads are borne in early summer. Height 45cm (18in), spread 60cm (2ft). It prefers a sunny position, and tolerates most soil conditions.

■ LEFT

LAGURUS OVATUS (HARE'S TAIL)

A hardy annual grass from southern Europe forming a compact clump. Height 60cm (2ft), spread 15cm (6in). The foliage is long and narrow and is topped by attractive fluffy white oval flower heads which make good dried flower arrangements. It prefers a free-draining soil in full sun, and may self-seed.

■ ABOVE
MILIUM EFFUSUM 'AUREUM' (BOWLES'
GOLDEN GRASS)

The species is a native of the northern hemisphere. This hardy,
yellow-green grass was made popular by E.A. Bowles. The foliage
is brightest in spring and reaches 30cm (1ft) high with loose, open
flower heads of the same colour in early summer, doubling the
overall height. Height 60cm (2ft), spread 45cm (18in). It prefers
light shade and is good for a woodland position where it is not
too dry. It has a tendency to self-seed.

■ ABOVE
MOLINIA CAERULEA SSP. *CAERULEA* 'VARIEGATA'
(VARIEGATED PURPLE MOOR GRASS)

A European and British grass that forms neat tufts of green and
white variegated leaves, sometimes tinged pink, that gently curve
down when mature. The foliage reaches a height of 30cm (1ft)
with loose, open, purple-grey flowers borne on stems in late
summer and autumn. Height and spread 60cm (2ft). It has good
yellow autumn colour. It tolerates most soil conditions and
situations, and is suitable for growing in pots.

■ LEFT
ORYZOPSIS LESSONIANA (RICE GRASS)

From the temperate regions of the northern hemisphere, this
grass forms neat clumps of fine, clear green foliage. Height and
spread 60cm (2ft). The stems bear delicate airy panicles. It
prefers a position in full sun in moisture-retentive soil.
O. miliacea is a taller species from the Mediterranean with
evergreen foliage and arching stems.

■ ABOVE LEFT

PENNISETUM ORIENTALE

A tender grass from south-west Asia and North Africa, it forms a clump of narrow leaves. Many spikes of soft, pinky-grey flowers appear in summer. Height and spread 60cm (2ft). It requires full sun and tolerates most soils, but is not fully hardy in colder areas and may need winter protection. The flower heads are useful for flower arranging and drying.

■ ABOVE RIGHT

PENNISETUM VILLOSUM

This north-east African plant has narrow leaves and whitish flower heads in summer, lasting well into autumn. Height and spread 60cm (2ft). Like *P. orientale* it is not fully hardy and will need winter protection in colder areas. The flower heads are useful for flower arranging and drying.

■ LEFT

STIPA TENUISSIMA

A native of Central and South America, this hardy grass has many needle-like leaves that grow from the base. Height and spread 60cm (2ft). The flowers are borne in summer, and are pale and lustrous with long hair-like filaments. The delicate stems and leaves become blond in late summer, and move in the lightest wind. It prefers well-drained soil and a sunny position.

Medium grasses

CALAMAGROSTIS X *ACUTIFLORA*
'OVERDAM' (VARIEGATED
FEATHER REED GRASS)

This is a variegated grass (the species is from
the northern hemisphere) that is smaller in
form than the popular *C.* x *acutiflora* 'Karl
Foerster'. The foliage is variegated with
white stripes, and makes an attractive
mound below the taller flowers. The stems
are upright and the flowers are borne in
early summer. Height to 1m (3ft), spread
60cm (2ft). It is hardy and tolerates most
soil conditions, and is best situated in
sun or partial shade.

CAREX FLAGELLIFERA

A hardy New Zealand sedge with arching stems of
bronze-brown, making a rounded clump. Height and
spread 70cm (28in). The flowers are inconspicuous.
It prefers a moist soil and will tolerate full sun to
partial shade. The unusual colour of its foliage
creates an interesting contrast with green, silver or
golden leaved plants.

*CAREX
PENDULA*
(WEEPING
SEDGE)

A hardy native of the
British Isles and most
of Europe, this grass
has evergreen foliage
from which taller
flowering stems
appear in spring and
early summer. The
flowers hang down
from the stems and
are dark brown.
Height and spread
1m (3ft). It prefers
moist soil and partial
shade, often occurring
in woodland. Its
attractive drooping
flowers make it useful
for flower arranging.

■ RIGHT
CYPERUS
INVOLUCRATUS, SYN.
C. ALTERNIFOLIUS

This tender Madagascan
evergreen requires a
minimum temperature of
about 5°C (41°F), and can
be grown in a conservatory.
Its tall stems bear arching,
leaf-like bracts and round
sprays of small, pale green
flowers. Height to 70cm
(28in), spread 30cm (1ft).
It prefers a sunny position
and very moist soil. The
dwarf form *C. involucratus*
'Nana' grows to about
half the height.

■ BELOW LEFT
CYPERUS LONGUS (GALINGALE)

This attractive European and North American species of
Cyperus is generally hardier than most, surviving winter
temperatures of about –15°C (5°F). It has umbrella-like
flower heads of greeny-brown. Height 1m (3ft), spread
45cm (18in). It tolerates moisture-retentive soils and can
be grown as a water marginal, preferring a sunny position.

■ BELOW RIGHT
DESCHAMPSIA CESPITOSA (TUFTED HAIR
GRASS, TUSSOCK GRASS)

A native of temperate areas in Europe and Asia, this hardy
grass forms dense fountains of leaves. The flowers are silky
and pale green at first, opening to airy seed heads of buff-
yellow. The panicle tends to fall to one side of the stem in
a graceful arch. Height 1.2m (4ft), spread 60cm (2ft). It
prefers moist soil in partial shade. The flower stems are
useful for flower arranging and drying.

■ ABOVE LEFT
GLYCERIA MAXIMA 'VARIEGATA'

From Britain, Europe and temperate areas of Asia, this hardy, variegated herbaceous grass has creamy-white and green striped leaves, with pink tints in spring. The leaves are broad and arching, and pale green flowers are borne above the foliage in summer. Height 1m (3ft), spread indefinite. It prefers moist soil in sun or partial shade. It spreads quickly and can be invasive.

■ ABOVE RIGHT
HELICTOTRICHON SEMPERVIRENS (BLUE OAT GRASS)

From south-west Europe, this grass has spiky, steely-blue leaves. The foliage is evergreen and loose flower heads are borne in early summer above the foliage. Height 1m (3ft), spread 60cm (2ft). Hardy in most areas, it requires full sun and a well-drained soil. It is suitable for growing in containers.

■ ABOVE
HYSTRIX PATULA (BOTTLE BRUSH GRASS)

A hardy North American grass with reddish-brown foliage in spring, becoming green as it matures. The flowers are borne in summer and have a distinctive bottle-brush appearance. Height 1m (3ft), spread 60cm (2ft). It prefers sun or part shade in most soil conditions. The flower heads are useful for flower arranging and drying.

■ RIGHT
IMPERATA CYLINDRICA 'RUBRA', SYN. *I. RUBRA* 'RED BARON' (JAPANESE BOOD GRASS)

A hardy, upright, Japanese grass with green leaves turning red from the tips. The foliage grows 60cm (2ft) high and the flowers are borne above the foliage in late summer. Height 1m (3ft), spread 60cm (2ft) or more. It tolerates most soil conditions but prefers moisture-retentive ground. Remove seed heads to prevent self-seeding (and reversion to plain green). It grows in sun or part shade.

■ BELOW LEFT
MELICA ALTISSIMA

Originating in Europe, this is a hardy, attractive grass with green foliage and stems. The pale flower heads bear a row of spikelets close together on one side of the stem. Height 1.2m (4ft), spread 60cm (2ft). It prefers sun or part shade and tolerates most soil conditions. It is useful for flower arranging and drying.

■ BELOW RIGHT
MISCANTHUS SINENSIS 'KLEINE FONTANE'

A cultivated variety of the species originating in southeast Asia, the name means 'Little Fountain'. Similar to *M. sinensis* 'Flamingo', it has paler pink flower heads borne in late summer. It makes a hardy upright clump and looks beautiful when planted in drifts through a border. Height 1m (3ft), spread 45cm (18in). It prefers a sunny position and tolerates most soil conditions.

■ RIGHT
*MOLINIA
CAERULEA
(PURPLE
MOOR GRASS)*

A native of
European
moorlands, this
grass has upright
stems topped with
tight purplish flower
heads in late
summer that last to
autumn. The foliage
is green, with good
yellow autumn
colour. Height 1.2m
(4ft), spread 60cm
(2ft). It is hardy and
prefers a moisture-
retentive, acid to
neutral soil in sun or
partial shade. This is
a useful plant for
inhospitable upland
situations.

■ ABOVE RIGHT
PLEIOBLASTUS AURICOMUS, SYN. *P.
VIRIDISTRIATUS*

A hardy Japanese bamboo that is useful for smaller gardens as it has
a height and spread of only 1m (3ft). It has golden foliage striped
with green, and the young sheaths and leaves are velvety in texture.
It prefers a moisture-retentive soil in sun or part shade, and is
suitable for growing in containers if kept well watered. *P. variegatus*
has bold green and white variegation, and grows to 60cm (2ft).

■ LEFT
PENNISETUM ALOPECUROIDES (FOUNTAIN
GRASS)

An east Asian and east Australian grass. It has narrow leaves that form
an attractive airy clump from which hairy, purple-brown, bottle-
brush-shaped flower heads emerge in the autumn. The good autumn
reddish-orange colour fades to buff in winter. It keeps its form well
out of season. Height and spread 1m (3ft). Hardy in most areas, it
prefers a sunny position and tolerates most soil types.

■ LEFT
POA LABILLARDIERI

A hardy Australian grass that forms dense mounds of fine blue-grey leaves above which the flowers are borne. The purplish flower heads open on stems that arch outwards, and appear in summer. The foliage is evergreen. Height 1.2m (4ft), spread 1m (3ft). It prefers full sun and a well-drained soil, and associates well with red or purple foliage.

■ BELOW
SHIBATAEA KUMASASA

A native of south-east Asia, this is a compact variety of bamboo, suitable for smaller gardens. Height 1m (3ft), spread 60cm (2ft); it tends to spread slowly. The leaves are broad and evergreen. It tolerates most positions, and prefers a moisture-retentive soil.

■ RIGHT
SCIRPOIDES HOLOSCHOENUS, SYN. SCIRPUS HOLOSCHOENUS, HOLOSCHOENUS VULGARIS

This European and south-west Asian member of the Cyperus (Rush) family has narrow, grass-like foliage that has good tawny autumn colour. The small brown flowers are borne close to the stems in clusters. It prefers a moisture-retentive soil, and is a useful marginal for growing at the water's edge in full sun or partial shade. Height to 1m (3ft), spread indefinite.

■ ABOVE

STIPA ARUNDINACEA

This hardy New Zealand grass has long, tawny foliage that intensifies in colour as winter approaches. The brownish flowers are borne in late summer on fine stems. Height and spread 1m (3ft). It prefers a moisture-retentive soil but will tolerate most soils, and grows well in a shady position.

■ ABOVE

STIPA CALAMAGROSTIS

A native of southern Europe, it has narrow, arching leaves. The long, silky flower heads arch out and are green with a reddish tinge fading to pale gold in late summer. The summer flowers last through the winter. Height and spread 1m (3ft). It prefers full sun and well-drained soil. One of the most attractive grasses that looks best massed in large clumps, it is useful for flower arranging and drying.

■ LEFT

STIPA BRACHYTRICHA (KOREAN FEATHER GRASS)

An attractive Korean grass with upright slender stems, topped by feathery, purple-pink flower heads. The foliage forms green clumps with golden autumn colour. Height 1.2m (4ft), spread 30cm (1ft). It tolerates most soil conditions, and prefers a sunny site. The attractive flowers make this a useful grass for flower arranging and drying.

Large grasses

■ RIGHT

ARUNDO DONAX (GIANT REED)

This tall, hardy, imposing southern
European grass has stout stems with broad,
blue-green leaves hanging down. It does
not usually flower in northern climates.
Height 2.5m (8ft), spread 60cm (2ft).
It requires a moist soil with adequate
drainage and a sunny position. The
variegated form *A. donax* var. *versicolor*
(syn. *A. donax* 'Variegata') has creamy
white striped foliage and is tender.

■ ABOVE RIGHT

CALAMAGROSTIS x *ACUTIFLORA*
'KARL FOERSTER' (FEATHER
REED GRASS)

This is a cultivated hardy hybrid of the northern
hemisphere species *C. arundinacea* and *C. epigejos*,
and is named after the influential German plantsman
Karl Foerster. The stems are strongly vertical and
slender, bearing flowers that turn reddish-brown
in late summer and fade through the winter. The
flowers are borne well above the leaves. Height 2m
(6ft), spread 60cm (2ft). It tolerates most soils
and prefers sun or partial shade. It should be cut
back in early spring.

■ LEFT

CHUSQUEA CULEOU

This species originated in Chile and is sometimes called
the Chilean bamboo. A hardy evergreen mass of small
leaves, it forms a dense clump which is generally slow
growing. Height and spread 5m (15ft). The culms are
an attractive olive-green colour when mature, with
younger culms being paler. This bamboo is unique in
having solid culms. It tolerates most soil conditions.

■ RIGHT
CORTADERIA SELLOANA
'PUMILA' (PAMPAS GRASS)

A native of South America, this is a hardy, compact form. It has evergreen foliage that forms a dense, rounded clump. The stems are erect and bear large, cream coloured, plume-like flowers that last from late summer onwards. Height 1.5m (5ft), spread 1m (3ft). It prefers full sun and tolerates most soils.

■ ABOVE
CORTADERIA SELLOANA 'SUNNINGDALE SILVER'

A hardy cultivated variety of the species originating in South America. This pampas grass has many erect stems bearing creamy flower plumes in late summer and autumn. The foliage is evergreen, and forms large rounded clumps at the base of the flower stems. Height 2m (6ft), spread 1.2m (4ft). It grows best in an open position in well-drained soil.

■ ABOVE
FARGESIA NITIDA

Originating in southern central Asia, this hardy bamboo has green narrow leaves on narrow purplish stems. Height and spread 3m (10ft) or more. An evergreen, it prefers a position in light shade and good soil. It is sometimes called the Fountain bamboo as the culms arch over and are topped with abundant foliage.

■ LEFT
LEYMUS ARENARIUS (LYME GRASS)

Native through most of the northern hemisphere, this hardy grass's native habitat is coastal dunes where its creeping rhizomes stabilize the sands. The arching leaves are blue-grey. It grows up to 60cm (2ft) high, and the flower spikes are taller, up to 1.5m (5ft), of the same blue-grey, fading to yellow in autumn. Spread indefinite. Invasive, it prefers a sunny position and well-drained soil.

■ BELOW LEFT
MISCANTHUS SINENSIS 'GRACILLIMUS'

The species originates in south east Asia. This hardy variety is a tall, clump-forming grass that can reach 1.5m (5ft) high. The foliage is narrow and curls towards the tips. The flowers are borne in plumes in autumn, and fade to an attractive, buff-yellow colour. It tolerates most soil types in sun or partial shade.

■ BELOW RIGHT
MISCANTHUS SINENSIS 'ZEBRINUS'

This hardy variety has narrow green leaves with horizontal bands of yellow variegation and silky brown flowers. Height 1.5m (5ft), spread 60cm (2ft). *M. sinensis* 'Strictus' is a similar variety, but has a more upright form and reaches 1.2m (4ft).

■ RIGHT
PHALARIS ARUNDINACEA VAR. PICTA 'PICTA' (RIBBON GRASS, GARDENER'S GARTERS)

From Europe and North America, this hardy evergreen grass has variegated green and white leaves reaching a height of 60cm (2ft) or more. The flower spikes are borne in summer and can be 1.5m (5ft) high; spread indefinite. Its native habitat is damp areas and water margins, but it grows well in most soil conditions in sun or part shade. It spreads rapidly with creeping rhizomes. *P. arundinacea* var. *picta* 'Tricolor' has variegated foliage tinged pink.

■ ABOVE
PHYLLOSTACHYS NIGRA (BLACK BAMBOO)

This hardy Chinese bamboo has culms that become black with age, making an interesting contrast with the foliage. The foliage is abundant and evergreen in most areas, although it may need winter protection in colder regions. Height 5m (15ft), spread 2m (6ft) or more. It performs best in a sunny position. An attractive bamboo for specimen planting.

■ RIGHT
PHYLLOSTACHYS BAMBUSOIDES (GIANT TIMBER BAMBOO)

An imposing hardy Chinese bamboo. When mature it has thick green culms that are used for building. The leaves are broad and densely borne. Height and spread 5m (15ft) or more. It prefers a rich soil so needs regular feeding. It tolerates most conditions in sun or partial shade. *P. bambusoides* 'Allgold' (syn. *P. bambusoides* 'Sulphurea') has yellow culms, sometimes with green stripes.

■ RIGHT
*PHYLLOSTACHYS
NIGRA* 'BORYANA'

A hardy bamboo (from a Chinese species) that makes an imposing stand. It has characteristic brown markings on its mature culms. The foliage is abundant and evergreen. Height 5m (15ft), spread 2m (6ft) or more. It prefers a rich, moisture-retentive soil in a sheltered position in sun or part shade. *P. nigra* f. *punctata* has darker brown markings on its culms.

■ BELOW LEFT
PHYLLOSTACHYS NIGRA VAR. *HENONIS*

This hardy bamboo (from a Chinese species) makes an upright clump. The tall culms are green when immature, aging to an attractive yellow-green. The foliage is abundant with many smallish, evergreen leaves giving a dense, bushy appearance. Height 5m (15ft), spread 2m (6ft) or more. It prefers a rich, moisture-retentive soil, and a sunny or partially shaded position.

■ BELOW RIGHT
PHYLLOSTACHYS VIRIDIGLAUCESCENS

An elegant hardy Chinese bamboo with dense green foliage. The culms are a smooth olive-green and may bend outwards with age. Height and spread 4m (12ft). It prefers a rich moist soil and sun or partial shade, and spreads easily in suitable conditions.

■ LEFT

PLEIOBLASTUS SIMONII F. *VARIEGATUS*

Originating in Japan, and previously known as *P. simonii* 'Heterophyllus', this is a tall, hardy bamboo reaching a height and spread of 4m (12ft) or more. The foliage is variegated with narrow green and white stripes, with the best variegation appearing on the younger growth. It makes an imposing stand, and associates well with large leaved plants. It tolerates most soils in sun or partial shade, but it may need winter protection in colder areas.

■ ABOVE
PSEUDOSASA JAPONICA (ARROW BAMBOO, METAKE)

The tall, erect culms of this hardy Japanese bamboo grow to 4m (12ft) high, and arch at the ends. Spread 4m (12ft) or more. The leaves are large, broad and evergreen, and the sheaths can last on the culms for several seasons. It tolerates most soil conditions, and prefers sun or part shade. A robust plant and a slow spreader.

■ ABOVE
SASA PALMATA

This attractive, hardy Japanese bamboo has broad, palmate green leaves. The culms form a spreading clump with strong evergreen foliage. Height 4m (12ft), spread indefinite. It prefers a position in partial shade and moisture-retentive soil.

■ BELOW
SASA VEITCHII

This hardy Japanese evergreen bamboo has broad, palmate leaves on purple stems. The leaves develop a distinctive creamy-buff margin. Height 1.5m (5ft), spread indefinite. It tolerates most soil conditions, preferring sun or part shade, and can be invasive, forming a dense thicket.

■ ABOVE
SEMIARUNDINARIA FASTUOSA

An imposing, upright Japanese bamboo with tall green culms that turn reddish-brown in maturity, it forms an erect stand topped with leafy foliage. Height 5m (15ft), spread indefinite. One of the hardiest bamboos, it will tolerate temperatures of –18°C (0°F). It prefers a rich, moisture-retentive soil in sun or partial shade.

■ LEFT
SORGHUM HALAPENSE (JOHNSON GRASS)

A Mediterranean grass that may require winter protection. It has plentiful foliage which is variegated with a white central stripe. The flower heads are open and arching, turning pinkish-brown in late summer and early autumn. Height 1.5m (5ft), spread 60cm (2ft). It prefers full sun and a rich, moisture-retentive soil.

■ LEFT
STIPA GIGANTEA (GIANT FEATHER GRASS)

A hardy Iberian grass with tall stems topped with open, oat-like flowers that become golden yellow, and last through the summer into autumn. The foliage forms a mound of tough leaves at the base of the stems. Height to 2m (6ft), spread indefinite. It prefers well-drained soil and a sunny position.

■ ABOVE LEFT
SPARTINA PECTINATA 'AUREOMARGINATA' (PRAIRIE CORD GRASS)

This hardy grass (from a North American species) has arching leaves that are yellow at the margins. In summer the flower spikes are pendulous with purple stamens. Height 2m (6ft), spread indefinite. It tolerates most conditions, but prefers a moisture-retentive soil in sun or part shade. It provides good autumn colour but can be an invasive spreader.

■ LEFT
TYPHA LATIFOLIA (BULRUSH, GREAT REEDMACE)

One of the most attractive, hardy marginal plants with upright foliage from Europe, Asia and North America. The erect stems are topped by compact, brown velvety flower heads in summer. It may be invasive so requires careful siting. It also needs a very moist soil or shallow water in sun or partial shade. It is valued for flower arranging and drying. Height to 2m (6ft), spread indefinite. *T. minima* (Dwarf reedmace) is a smaller variety more suitable for gardens where space is limited.

The Grower's Guide

Buying grasses

As grasses and bamboos have increased in popularity, more nurseries and garden centres are stocking them, and the available choice is constantly widening. Garden centres often stock several varieties, and tend to be more expensive than nurseries, where the plants have often been grown from seed, or propagated on site. There are a few specialist nurseries, which generally have a wider choice. You may be lucky and have one close by; if not, it is worth purchasing by mail order.

Before buying a grass remember to check on the general health of the plant. The foliage should be springy and colourful but not too dense, which could indicate that the plant has already become congested. New growth should be emerging at the appropriate season. Unless the plant is dying back naturally in the autumn, avoid unhealthy grasses with brown foliage. If possible, check the root system of the plant by slipping it out of its container, and reject any that have a congested root system as they are difficult to establish. Also reject a plant if the soil in the container falls away from the roots, which might indicate that the plant

is not yet mature enough for planting out. Ideally, the root system should bind the soil, and be visibly healthy without being overcrowded.

You should avoid buying plants in soil that has dried out, for the lack of water is likely to have caused them

■ RIGHT
A well-stocked nursery sales area with a wide range of grasses. Carefully read the information panel for each variety to ensure that the grass will be suitable for your garden.

distress. And unless the soil is thoroughly re-wetted before planting, the grass will be difficult to establish (peat-based composts or soil mixes are particularly prone to this). Probably the best method of re-wetting dried soil is to plunge the container into a bucket of water and

hold it down until the air bubbles have finished rising to the surface. Then lift the container out of the bucket and allow the excess water to drain away. The container should feel noticeably heavier because of the water absorbed by the soil.

You must also check that the plant has not been over-watered as this can cause the foliage to rot. Leaves in this condition are dark brown at the base and easily come away from the rest of the plant. In severe cases the plant may not recover. Grasses that prefer a well-drained soil are particularly vulnerable to this problem.

When buying grasses consider the ultimate height and spread of the plant, and whether it is suitable for

the location you have in mind. Bear in mind the aspect and soil of your site, and choose a plant that will cope with that environment – the information panel for each grass will indicate whether it is suitable.

GRASSES THAT TOLERATE SHADE

Carex hachijoensis 'Evergold'

Carex pendula

Deschampsia cespitosa varieties

Fargesia nitida

Hakonechloa macra 'Alboaurea'

Milium effusum 'Aureum'

Stipa arundinacea

GRASSES FOR SUNNY POSITIONS

Cortaderia selloana varieties

Festuca glauca varieties

Helictotrichon sempervirens

Koeleria glauca

Leymus arenarius

Pennisetum varieties

Stipa calamagrostis

Stipa tenuissima

Uncinia rubra

Growing from seed

■ BELOW
Stipa splendens provides an attractive
display of flower heads for seed-taking
in late summer.

This method of propagation is more
suitable for species grasses than for
cultivated varieties, which do not
generally come true from seed. For
this reason cultivated varieties are best
propagated by division. Seeds taken
from these however may result in
some interesting new seedlings, but
this cannot be guaranteed. Some
grasses self-seed readily, such as
Milium effusum 'Aureum' (which is a
cultivated variety that *does* come true
from seed) and *Stipa tenuissima*. The

seedlings of these plants can be
transplanted in the open ground or in
containers. To prevent unwanted self-
seeding remove the flower heads
before the seeds have a chance to
form. Bamboos flower far less
frequently than true grasses, and are
best propagated by division.

Ripe seed can be collected from
the flower heads and stored in a cool
dry place, but the best results are
achieved from seeds sown straight
after collection. Seeds taken from

spring-flowering grasses and sown
straight away will produce new plants
from late summer to early autumn.
Seeds sown immediately from later
flowering grasses will produce new
plants the following spring.

The size of seeds varies between
grasses. Larger seeds, such as those
from *Hystrix patula*, can be placed
individually on to a bed of potting
soil, whereas smaller seeds, such as
those from *Milium effusum* 'Aureum'
can be sprinkled on to the potting

TAKING AND SOWING SEED

1 Carefully collect the ripe seed by gently running your fingers up the flower stem.

2 Fill a container three-quarters full with potting soil, and sow the seeds evenly on the surface.

3 Cover the seeds with a layer of soil about 1cm (¹/2 inch) deep.

4 Cover the soil with a layer of fine gravel to prevent water loss through evaporation.

5 Water well initially, but take care not to overwater as this can cause the seeds to rot.

soil. They will produce a mass of new seedlings in due course which can then be divided into clumps of several plantlets, and potted on into separate containers.

Once the seeds have been sown the container can be left outside, or placed in a cold frame to germinate.

Outdoors in dry periods, or under cover, the container should be watered, but take care not to overwater as this could cause the seeds to rot and fail. Covering the container with grit will provide extra winter protection for seed sown late in the season.

6 When the seeds have germinated and new growth is well established the grass can be planted out.

Dividing grasses

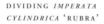

Division is a useful way of propagating grasses, especially cultivated varieties that may not come true from seed. Bamboos are best propagated by division because they flower very infrequently, so seed is hard to come by.

Division is also necessary if the grass has become congested. One sign of congestion is a dense mass of stems rising from the centre of the plant, with the base of the plant appearing to be raised into a hummock. The older foliage may become brown and unattractive, and even die off. Division and

1 The grass now fills its container and is ready for repotting or dividing.

2 Remove the plant from its container or, if it is planted in the ground, dig it up taking care to keep the root system intact. Carefully separate the plant into sections ensuring that each part has foliage and root systems. This can be done by hand as here or by using the edge of a spade or an axe for tougher plants.

3 Plant each new section in a container slightly larger than its root system, or replant directly into the ground.

4 Cut back the foliage to discourage pests and diseases, and to encourage new growth.

5 Divisions that have been potted up. When they become established and have new growth they can be repotted or planted out.

replanting will create more space for the plant and encourage new healthy growth.

Grasses planted in containers may become congested in this way, with the root system tightly packing the pot. When dividing such plants it is best to tease out the congested roots before replanting to encourage them to spread outwards, and not continue in a downward spiral. In cases of severe root congestion it may be necessary to divide the plant using a sharp spade, axe or saw. This may also be necessary when dividing bamboos that have tough rhizomes.

■ LEFT
Some grasses such as this pampas grass have sharp edges to their leaves. Gloves should be worn when handling.

■ BELOW LEFT
This small bamboo *Pleio blastus auricomus* can be divided to produce new plants. Make sure that each group of stems has roots and rhizomes before replanting.

Some grasses may be divided in the autumn when the plant has ceased to put on new growth for the season; the warm soil and moist air will help the new plants become established. Cut back the foliage after division, and new growth will appear the following spring. Preferably, division should take place in the spring, ideally just before new growth starts to prevent it from being damaged when you slice the clump apart. In either case, when dividing grasses always cut out the dead or unhealthy growth to create a more healthy and attractive-looking plant.

■ BOTTOM LEFT
Molinia caerulea ssp. *caerulea* 'Variegata'
and *Rudbeckia* make an appealing duo in
this perennial border.

General maintenance

The maintenance requirements of
grasses are low. Once established they
require very little attention as they are
generally pest and disease free.
However, to ensure that your grasses
look their best some minor routine
maintenance is advisable.

Grooming

This is particularly relevant to
evergreen grasses such as *Festuca
glauca*. As new growth is produced
some of the old growth dies back
naturally, turning brown. This old
growth is best removed as it is not
only unsightly, but can also harbour

COMBING OUT OLD GROWTH

Run your fingers through the grass to
remove the dead foliage. Wear protective
gloves for grasses that have sharp edges to
their leaves to prevent cuts.

pests and diseases. By running your
fingers gently and firmly through the
foliage much of the dead growth can
be easily removed. It may be
necessary to then pluck out the
individual leaves that come away less
easily. Take care not to damage any
new growth. This exercise is best
carried out in the spring to create
space for new growth, and to freshen
your plant's appearance for the new
season. Grooming can take place at
any time, but if your plant requires
excess care it may be a sign that it
needs to be divided or repotted.

Cutting back

Once the foliage of a herbaceous grass
has faded it may take on a ghostly
appearance, while maintaining much
of its structure. Where this occurs
you may prefer to leave the foliage
through the winter, only cutting back
the old foliage next spring as new
growth emerges, or earlier if the
foliage collapses. Some grasses,
however, lose their form when they
die back in the autumn, and they are
best cut back then to discourage pests
and diseases. Fresh new growth will
emerge the following spring.

The bamboo *Pleioblastus auricomus*
benefits from being cut back in early

■ BELOW
Contrasting grass flower heads and foliage
provide an attractive grouping.

spring to encourage bright new
foliage, otherwise bamboos do not
usually need cutting back except to
remove dead, damaged or weak
growth, or to reduce their height.

The traditional way to rejuvenate
Cortaderia selloana is to burn off the
foliage, but this should be carefully
managed to prevent the fire getting
out of hand. Also note that this and
many grasses have sharp edges to
their foliage which can cause cuts to
the hands. Wear protective gloves
to prevent accidents.

CUTTING BACK GRASS IN THE AUTUMN

1 In autumn the foliage of herbaceous
grasses begins to die back. When
the leaves collapse and turn brown they
can be removed.

2 Using a pair of sharp secateurs
(pruners) cut off the leaves near the
base. When cutting back in spring take
care not to damage new growth.

3 Remove the cut foliage to discourage
any pests and diseases. From this
neat clump new growth will emerge
in the spring.

Planting grasses

The best time for planting grasses is in the spring or autumn. Those which are susceptible to low temperatures are best planted in the spring so that they can become established over the summer. However, planting can also take place in suitable conditions in winter if the ground is not frozen or waterlogged. With spring and summer planting it is important to keep the plants well watered to guard against drying out.

Whenever you do decide to plant the grass it should be watered beforehand. To ensure that the roots are thoroughly soaked, plunge the

---

GRASSES FOR MOIST SOILS

Acorus gramineus 'Variegatus'
Bamboos (most species)
Carex hachijoensis 'Evergold'
Carex elata 'Aurea'
Cyperus longifolius
Glyceria maxima 'Variegata'
Juncus effusus 'Spiralis'
Miscanthus sinensis varieties
Molinia caerulea ssp. *caerulea* 'Variegata'
Scirpoides holoschoenus
Typha latifolia

---

plant in its container into a bucket of water until the bubbles stop rising. Then remove the plant and allow it to drain.

Ground preparation is equally important. Ideally grasses should have conditions similar to their native habitat. If conditions are not ideal, you can improve the situation. When planting a grass that prefers a well-drained soil, you can incorporate some grit to improve the drainage. This is especially beneficial where the soil is heavy and moisture-retentive.

For grasses that require a moisture-retentive soil, add plenty of

---

PLANTING A GRASS

1 Prepare the ground by digging a hole for the grass. The hole should be approximately twice the size of the plant's container.

2 Sprinkle some fertilizer into the hole and blend in a little with the soil. Wear gloves if recommended by the manufacturer. Water the grass while it is in its container. If the soil has dried out, immerse the pot in a bucket of water until the air bubbles stop rising.

■ BELOW
Stipa calamagrostis makes an ideal
companion for sedum in a sunny border.

organic matter – peat, spent
mushroom compost and garden
compost are fine. Moisture loss
through evaporation can be reduced
by applying a mulch around the grass
after planting. Mulches such as bark
chips and gravel look best when
covering an entire bed, whereas peat
or ground cocoa shells are of finer
texture and blend in with the
surrounding soil, and can be applied
just to the immediate planting area.

A little fertilizer applied at the
time of planting will give the grass a
boost. Thereafter no additional
feeding is necessary; too rich a soil

can cause lush, lax growth. When
planting ensure that there is enough
space for the grass to spread. Some
grasses and bamboos have invasive
underground rhizomes that can
spread over a wide area, sending up
new shoots. They should be
contained by sinking an impenetrable
barrier such as old roof slates or metal
sheeting around the roots. After
planting, water the grass well until
it is established. Thereafter, in
normal conditions watering should
not be necessary if the grass has been
sited in a suitable position for its
type, and a mulch applied.

3 Remove the grass from its container and place it in the centre of
the hole, and fill in with soil. Firm the soil around the grass to
stabilize it, and to eliminate any large air pockets.

4 Water well and continue to water regularly until the plant
is established.

Growing in containers

Many grasses are suitable for growing in pots as single specimens, or combined with other plants in larger containers. Where space is limited, growing grasses in containers is an ideal way to grow some of the more invasive types, although division

and repotting will be necessary in order to prevent the plant from becoming congested.

Grouping planted containers together can form a versatile display for a terrace or balcony. Try a combination of grasses and hostas

with shrubs such as box, hydrangea and euonymus to create an interesting composition of foliage plants. Bedding annuals can also be added to the group for seasonal colour.

Choose a suitable container for the grass you intend to plant. There are

PLANTING A CONTAINER

1 Before planting, submerge the plant in its container in a bucket of water until the air bubbles stop rising. Then allow to drain.

2 Cover the bottom of the container with pebbles or broken crocks to facilitate drainage.

3 Fill the container with potting soil, allowing the plant to sit approximately 2.5cm (1in) below the rim.

4 If the roots show signs of congestion, tease them out. Place the plant in the container and backfill with potting soil. Firm down the soil to secure the plant and eliminate any large air pockets.

5 Water well after planting.

6 Cover the soil with gravel or grit to help prevent water loss through evaporation.

■ BELOW
This mixed container planting includes
Stipa tenuissima to create an airy effect.

many shapes and sizes available in a variety of materials. It is fun to experiment with different types of grasses, in different shaped containers, to achieve a particular effect. Whatever the shape of pot, always make sure it is large enough to contain the grass, as well as allowing space for further growth. Grasses that are overcrowded have a distressed appearance with some foliage dying back as the roots are deprived of space and nutrients. Overcrowding of roots also makes the container dry out quickly, which makes frequent watering a necessity. When planting, gently tease out the roots if they show signs of congestion.

If you use a ceramic container and live in an area that is prone to frost, check on the frost resistance of the pot. Some terracotta pots are guaranteed frost-proof for up to 10 years, but note that they are usually more expensive than pots that are labelled frost resistant. Frost damage is dangerous because it can cause the pot to crack, exposing the roots to the elements, possibly killing tender plants.

Grasses grown in containers need regular watering. Those placed in sunny or windy positions will dry out more quickly than those placed in shade. Always consider the needs of the particular grass when watering: *Stipa tenuissima*, for example, is a plant that thrives in fairly dry conditions and does not like to be waterlogged, whereas *Carex elata* 'Aurea' prefers damp soil and must not be allowed to dry out. A layer of gravel or grit over the compost helps to prevent water loss through evaporation.

Drainage is equally important when planting in a container. Always ensure that the container has a hole in the base, and that the bottom is filled with stones or pieces of broken pots so that excess water can freely drain away. This can also be facilitated by standing the container on terracotta legs that raise it clear of the ground. Grasses that prefer free-draining conditions may rot at the base if insufficient drainage is provided.

It is not usually necessary to apply a fertilizer to grasses grown in containers. Many grasses come from areas of poor soil and are well able to cope with a paucity of nutrients. If the growing medium is too rich the plant may develop fleshy, lax foliage and look less attractive. Annual repotting into a larger container with fresh soil should provide sufficient nutrients for the following growing season.

GRASSES SUITABLE FOR GROWING IN CONTAINERS

Carex hachijoensis 'Evergold'

Carex elata 'Aurea'

Festuca glauca varieties

Hakonechloa macra 'Alboaurea'

Helictotrichon sempervirens

Imperata cylindrica 'Rubra'

Molinia caerulea ssp. *caerulea* 'Variegata'

Phyllostachys nigra

Pleioblastus auricomus

Pleioblastus variegatus

Drying grasses

Many grasses are suitable for dried flower arrangements, as they retain their flower and seed heads for long periods. Some grasses have highly ornamental flower heads which can add interest to a mixed arrangement of dried flowers, or look splendid on their own. Dried grasses are especially useful since they often fade to subtle tones of gold and buff.

As the season progresses grasses will dry naturally in the garden. They can be brought into the house without the need for further drying, though by this time the seed head may be too mature, causing it to

GRASSES WITH ATTRACTIVE FLOWER/SEED HEADS

Cortaderia selloana varieties
Deschampsia cespitosa varieties
Hordeum jubatum
Hystrix patula
Lagurus ovatus
Miscanthus sinensis varieties
Panicum capillare
Pennisetum orientale
Pennisetum villosum
Stipa calamagrostis
Stipa gigantea
Typha latifolia

TAKING GRASSES FOR DRYING

1 Use a sharp pair of secateurs (pruners) to cut the stem. Leave plenty of stem, as this can be trimmed later.

2 Remove any foliage attached to the stem.

3 Tie the grasses together using a slip knot. This can be tightened should the stems shrink in the drying process. Avoid tying more than five or six grasses together as they could become tangled and break when dried. Hang them upside down, or lay flat in a dry place.

4 Different effects can be achieved with drying. The silky flowers of this *Miscanthus* have opened into fluffy heads for use in an arrangement, or as a specimen on their own.

■ BELOW
The open panicles of *Stipa gigantea* rise
above this border planting, and make a
semi-transparent screen.

disintegrate. It is best to pick grasses
for drying when the seed head has
just formed, and in dry conditions.
Should the grasses be picked in wet
weather, blot away the excess
moisture with paper kitchen towel.

The grasses should then be tied
together and hung upside down in a

dry, airy, dark place, such as an airing
cupboard. Since it is important to
allow the air to circulate around the
grasses, several small bunches are
better than one large one. This also
helps prevent the dried seed heads
getting tangled and breaking. If you
wish to retain the curve of the stems,

dry the grasses upright in a vase. After
one to two weeks the grasses will be
dried and ready to use. Exposure
to sunlight will cause dried grasses
to fade. If you do not want this
effect, it is best to refresh your dried
flower arrangement with newly dried
grasses at least annually.

Arranging grasses

As well as being excellent garden plants, grasses are also invaluable for flower arranging. Grasses used in arrangements can have several effects. Ornamental seed heads add interest and their subtle tones offset other more colourful cut flowers. Try using the pinkish flowers of *Miscanthus sinensis* 'Flamingo' or *Miscanthus sinensis* 'Malepartus' with the rich reddish-bronze colours of *Sedum spectabile* 'Autumn Joy' (Ice plant) and *Euphorbia dulcis* 'Chameleon' in a late summer arrangement. Alternatively the bright yellow-green of

GRASSES WITH INTERESTING FOLIAGE

Elymus magellanicus

Hakonechloa macra 'Alboaurea'

Imperata cylindrica 'Rubra'

Juncus effusus 'Spiralis'

Milium effusum 'Aureum'

Miscanthus sinensis 'Zebrinus'

Molinia caerulea ssp. *caerulea* 'Variegata'

Phalaris arundinacea 'Tricolor'

Pleioblastus auricomus

Sasa veitchii

Milium effusum 'Aureum' in spring is ideal grouped with other spring flowers, especially those in the blue spectrum such as *Muscari armeniacum* (Grape hyacinth) and *Hyacinthoides non-scripta* (Bluebell).

The tall stems of some grasses are especially useful for adding height and width to an arrangement, and the light texture of the flowers gives an attractive airy feel that works well in both formal and informal arrangements. *Pennisetum alopecuroides* and *Stipa calamagrostis* have ornamental flower heads on longish

FLOWER ARRANGING WITH GRASSES

1 Fill the vase with water. Having chosen the flowers for your arrangement, strip off the lower leaves and cut off the ends of the stems immediately before placing them in the vase.

2 Begin your arrangement by placing the flower or foliage that creates the background to offset the other plants. Here the interesting foliage of *Euphorbia dulcis* 'Chameleon' has been used.

■ BELOW
This arrangement combines flower heads of complementary colours with *Miscanthus sinensis 'Malepartus'*.

stems, and both are a very good choice. For a large-scale arrangement try *Miscanthus sinensis* varieties and *Stipa gigantea*. For a smaller arrangement, such as a dining table centrepiece, cut the stems of larger grasses to suit the proportions of your arrangement, or use the flower heads from a relatively low-growing grass such as *Festuca glauca*.

The foliage of grasses can also be used effectively in flower arrangements. Consider the wide range of grasses with coloured and variegated foliage that can be incorporated with other cut flowers to achieve a graceful, airy effect. The foliage of grasses such as *Cortaderia selloana* 'Aureolineata' is interesting in itself, but its natural elegant curves will enhance the shape of an arrangement as it arches outwards. Wear gloves when handling the foliage for protection against the sharp edges.

Bamboo foliage and stems can be used in interesting arrangements too, perhaps with an oriental theme. Their upright stems create a strong vertical accent. The broad green leaves of the bamboos *Sasa palmata* and *Sasa veitchii* add unusual foliage effects where a more solid appearance is desired.

The best effects are usually achieved by using only two or three different types of flowers, so as not to confuse the eye with too many shapes and colours. Stems can be kept in place if secured in florist's foam, or roughly folded wire mesh, although the latter may scratch the surface of the vase.

3 A tall grass can create height and airiness. Use plants in odd numbers. This helps to make the arrangement roughly triangular, and has a balancing effect. Finally add the focal point of the arrangement; here the rich flowers of the ice plant attract the eye, and are set off by the coloured foliage and grass.

Calendar

Spring

Cut back herbaceous grasses that have held their form through the winter, and remove dead foliage that may harbour pests and diseases. Plant out new grasses in suitable conditions. Groom evergreen grasses to remove dead foliage. Continue to plant new stock. Divide any grasses that may have become congested and replant. Collect seed from spring-flowering grasses and sow in containers. Remove any unwanted new self-seeded plants from the garden before flowering. Repot any container-grown grasses that are in danger of becoming pot-bound.

■ ABOVE
Bamboo planted behind perennials gives an attractive vertical accent to this well-designed border.

■ BELOW
Some grasses such as this pampas grass retain their shape well in winter and create a stunning effect in the frost.

Summer

Water container-grown plants regularly, and any newly planted grasses that are not yet established. Collect seeds from summer-flowering plants and sow in containers.

Autumn

Continue to collect seeds from later flowering grasses for sowing. Divide grasses that have become congested through the year. Cut back herbaceous foliage that has died back. Plant new stock in suitable conditions. Protect tender specimens against hard frosts with garden fleece, bracken or straw. Continue to remove dead foliage.

Winter

Cut back any flowering stems if they collapse as the season progresses.

Other recommended grasses

Heights and spreads given at the end of the description are approximate measurements when the plant is mature.

Bambusa multiplex, syn. B. glaucescens (Hedge bamboo) A vigorous spreading, tall, evergreen plant from south-east Asia. Half-hardy, needing protection below 0°C (32°F). Grow in a conservatory. 15m (50ft) x indefinite in native conditions.

Bromus inermis

Bromus inermis This is a hardy grass from Europe and Asia with attractive feathery flower heads. Tolerates most soil conditions, needing a sunny position. *B. ramosus* has loose flowers on arching stems. 1m (3ft) x 60cm (2ft).

Carex dipsacea This attractive sedge grass originated in New Zealand. It has dark brown and olive-green foliage. The

flower-heads are also blackish-brown and are borne in mid- to late summer. A good plant to combine with golden foliage. Tolerates most soils in sun or part shade. 45cm (18in) x 45cm (18in).

Carex riparia 'Variegata'

Carex riparia 'Variegata' Hardy sedge species from the northern hemisphere with long, fine leaves that are variegated with white stripes. Requires moisture-retentive soil and a sunny position. Tends to spread. 60cm (2ft) x 60cm (2ft).

Chasmanthium latifolium (North American wild oats, Spangle grass, Sea oats) This hardy North American grass has abundant foliage that keeps its bright green colour in late summer, and fades to gold in the autumn. It makes a dense, upright clump. The flowers have flat, pendent panicles on upright stems

reaching 1m (3ft) high. It prefers a moisture-retentive soil in sun or partial shade. Excellent for drying. 45cm (18in) x 45cm (18in).

Cortaderia selloana 'Aureolineata' Hardy grass (species from South America) with variegated green and gold foliage in rounded mounds, with feathery flower spikes in late summer. Likes an open position in well drained soil. *C. selloana* 'Albolineata' is smaller, with white variegated foliage. 1.5m (5ft) x 1.2m (4ft).

Chasmanthium latifolium

Cyperus eragrostis, syn. C. vegetus, (American galingale) Hardy North American spreader with broad leaves and flowers of yellow-green in late summer and autumn. Tolerates most soil conditions, preferring sun or partial shade. 60cm (2ft) x 1m (3ft) or more.

Deschampsia cespitosa 'Goldtau', syn. D. cespitosa 'Golden Dew' Widely available hardy, smaller variety of *D. cespitosa*. The flower heads are more compact and turn to golden yellow in late summer. Another interesting variety is 'Bronzeschleier' ('Bronze Veil'). Dry to damp soil in sun or partial shade. 1m (3ft) x 60cm (2ft).

Cortaderia selloana 'Aureolineata'

Eragrostis curvula (African love grass, Weeping love grass) Grown as a fodder crop in southern Africa, it has slender foliage forming leafy clumps from which the flower heads rise to 1m (3ft). The flower heads are finely branched, with an attractive pale grey colour fading to parchment in the autumn. It prefers a poor soil and full sun, and may require winter protection in colder areas. 60cm (2ft) x 60cm (2ft).

Festuca eskia This is a low-growing, hardy, evergreen grass forming bright green mounds. It has loose green flowers in summer. It prefers an acid, well-drained soil in a sunny position. 30cm (1ft) x an indefinite spread.

Deschampsia cespitosa 'Goldtau'

Festuca glauca 'Blaufuchs', syn. *F. glauca* 'Blue Fox' The species originates in Europe. This hardy, cultivated variety has light blue-grey spiky foliage. It prefers well-drained soil in a sunny position. Comb out any dead foliage in early spring to maintain a good blue appearance. 20cm (8in) x 20cm (8in).

Festuca glauca 'Elijah Blue' Hardy evergreen grass, widely available, with foliage of a

good blue colour. Forms neat clumps with blue-grey flowers in early summer. Full sun and well-drained soil. 30cm (1ft) x 30cm (1ft).

Eragrostis curvula

Festuca glauca 'Golden Toupee' Similar to 'Elijah Blue' but with golden-green foliage. Forms a fine, rounded clump. Full sun and well-drained soil. 30cm (1ft) x 30cm (1ft).

Festuca vivipara A native of the uplands of northern Europe, this hardy blue-green grass makes a dense mound up to 25cm (10in) high, with the flower spikes born above the foliage to about 35cm (14in). The flowers are a delicate pinkish buff, and are borne in early to mid-summer. It prefers a sunny position and a moisture-retentive acidic soil. It is suitable for container planting. 35cm (14in) x 35cm (14in).

Holcus mollis 'Albovariegatus' Variegated form of *H. mollis* (Creeping soft grass), native of Britain and northern Europe. Soft textured grass in upright clumps. Leaves have a green central stripe and white margins. Pale green flowers. Tolerates most aspects and soils. 30cm (1ft) x indefinite.

Miscanthus sinensis 'Flamingo'

Juncus effusus 'Spiralis' (Corkscrew rush) Hardy, cultivated variety of the species found in most temperate regions. It has shiny green stems that spiral out from the centre. Full sun or part shade. 1.2m (4ft) x 1m (3ft).

Koeleria glauca Hardy, tuft-forming evergreen grass of low-growing habit from Europe and Asia. It has blue-grey foliage and pale upright flowers in summer.

It prefers full sun and well-drained soil. 30cm (1ft) x 30cm (1ft).

Luzula sylvatica (Greater woodrush) Originating in most parts of Europe, this hardy spreading perennial rush is good for naturalizing in woodland. It has grass-like foliage and small, brown flowers which are borne in loose open sprays. 60cm (2ft) x indefinite spread.

Miscanthus sinensis 'Variegatus'

Melica altissima 'Atropurpurea' Hardy grass (species from eastern Europe and central Asia). Foliage is tall and soft. Summer flowers are purple spikes set close to the stem. Prefers sun or partial shade and well-drained soil. 1m (3ft) x 60cm (2ft).

Miscanthus sacchariflorus Large hardy grass from eastern Asia with bamboo-like stems. Long leaves with a slender white central stripe. The flowers of silver-brown are not readily produced in cool climates. Tolerates most situations, but prefers moisture-retentive soils. Spreads slowly. 3m (10ft) x 3m (10ft) or more.

Molinia caerulea ssp. *arundinacea*

Miscanthus sinensis 'Flamingo' A shorter culti-vated variety of the hardy, south-east Asian species. The foliage is narrow, topped by upright stems. The many flower heads are lustrous pink. Prefers a moisture-retentive soil in full sun. 1m (3ft) x 45cm (18in).

Miscanthus sinensis 'Malepartus' This garden variety of the species from south-east Asia has tall stems topped with silky pinkish flower-heads in late summer. It tolerates most soils in sun or part

shade. The flower heads are good for drying as they become a fluffy pinkish-grey. 2m (6ft) or more x 60cm (2ft).

Miscanthus sinensis 'Morning Light' Variegated foliage giving a graceful, shimmering effect. Panicles of flowers in early autumn. Tolerates most soils in sun or partial shade. 1.2m (4ft) x 60cm (2ft).

Nassella trichotoma

Miscanthus sinensis var. *purpurascens* Originating from south-east Asia, this variety has brownish-purple foliage with a fine white central stripe and good autumn colour. The pinkish flower heads are borne on upright stems. Tolerates most soils in sun or partial shade. 1.5m (5ft) x 60cm (2ft).

Miscanthus sinensis 'Silberfeder', syn. *M. sinensis* 'Silver Feather' Tall, upright stems with feathery flowers of

lustrous, pale pinkish-bronze in late summer. The stems can remain upright through winter. Prefers full sun to light shade and tolerates most soils. 2m (6ft) x 60cm (2ft).

Miscanthus sinensis 'Variegatus' The leaves are relatively broad and have several bold green and white stripes making a stunning effect against a dark background. Autumn flowers. Prefers a moisture-retentive soil in full sun. 1.5m (5ft) x 60cm (2ft).

Panicum virgatum

Molinia caerulea ssp. *arundinacea* (Tall purple moor grass) A hardy grass from European and British species. The foliage forms a neat clump of stiff leaves with fine, upright stems bearing loose purple flowers in late summer and autumn. It tolerates most soils. 2m (6ft) x 1m (3ft).

Molinia caerulea ssp. *caerulea* 'Edith Dudzus' Cultivated grass from European and British species. Fine and narrow, bright green foliage. Dark flowering spikes appear above the leaves. Prefers a moist soil, and full sun to partial shade. 60cm (2ft) x 45cm (18in).

Phalaris aquatica

Nassella trichotoma Hardy South American grass with fine leaves and delicate pinkish stems, reaching a height of 60cm (2ft). Many tiny, airy flowers are borne in summer and appear like spun threads over the foliage. It prefers a moist soil and a sunny position. The flower heads are useful for dried flower arrangements. 60cm (2ft) x 60cm (2ft).

Panicum capillare (Witch grass) Tender, annual North American grass with broad green leaves. The stems bear dense sprays of pale green spikelets. Sown from seed each year. Tolerates most soils and does best in full sun. 1m (3ft) x 30cm (1ft).

Phyllostachys nidularia

Panicum virgatum (Switch grass) Originating in North America, this perennial grass produces a mass of fine flower heads that spread gracefully over the arching green foliage. Tolerates most soil conditions in a sunny position. 1.2m (4ft) x 60cm (2ft).

Pennisetum alopecuroides 'Hameln' (Dwarf fountain grass) A cultivated variety of the widespread species that forms an arching clump up to 60cm (2ft) high, it is useful for smaller gardens or for the front of the border. Fluffy flower heads appear in late summer, lasting into autumn. It prefers well-drained soil and a sunny position. As with the species, the flower heads

are useful for flower arranging and drying. 60cm (2ft) x 60cm (2ft).

Pennisetum incomptum (Spreading fountain grass) Hardy grass from south-east Asia with narrow, light green foliage topped by stems bearing pale flower heads. Prefers a sunny position and tolerates most soil types but is invasive. There is a purple form with purple-brown flower heads. 1.2m (4ft) x indefinite.

Stipa gigantea

Phalaris aquatica This attractive perennial grass originated in the Mediterranean. It has dense cylindrical flower heads that turn buff-yellow in late summer. The foliage is blue-green and forms tufts around the base of the flower stems. It is hardy and prefers moisture-retentive soil in sun or part shade. 1.2m (4ft) x indefinite spread.

Phyllostachys aurea Originating in China, this is a bamboo with yellow-green culms. It has smallish narrow leaves of mid- to light green that are set off well against a dark background such as a yew hedge. Prefers a rich moisture retentive soil in sun or part shade. It is suitable for growing in containers. 4m (12ft) x 2m (6ft).

Stipa lepida

Phyllostachys nidularia Hardy Chinese bamboo that makes a dense, bushy clump. The culms are yellow-green, fringed with foliage almost to ground level. Good for screening in a sheltered position. Prefers a rich, moisture-retentive soil in sun or partial shade. 3–5m (9–15ft) x 3m (9ft) or more.

Poa chaixii (Broad-leaved meadow grass, Chaix's meadow grass) Hardy European and south-west Asian grass. The leaves are

broad and green, and the loose flower heads are also green. Prefers shade at the margins of woodland. Tolerates most soil conditions. 1m (3ft) x 1m (3ft).

Stipa splendens (Chee grass) A grass from central Asia that forms an arching, rounded clump of fine foliage, topped by feathery flower heads that turn golden-buff. It prefers a sunny position and tolerates most soil types. 1.5m (5ft) x 1.2m (4ft).

Uncinia rubra (Hook sedge) This New Zealand sedge has attractive, narrow reddish-brown leaves up to a height of 45cm (18in). The foliage fades from the tips in winter to a parchment-like colour. It requires well-drained soil and does best in a sunny position. Though hardy, it may be slow to recover after a cold winter, especially on heavy soil. 45cm (18in) x 45cm (18in).

Stipa splendens

Index

ACKNOWLEDGEMENTS

The author and publishers would like to thank the following people for their help in the production of his book: Trevor Scott; Jonathan Buckley; Beth Chatto; Bodiam Nursery, Robertsbridge, E. Sussex; Caroline and Jerry Taylor, Wendover; Christopher Lloyd; Cambridge Botanical Gardens; Wisley Gardens. The following photographs were taken at Beth Chatto's garden: pp.1, 6, 7, 8, 10, 12t, 13b, 23bl, 23br, 30t, 32t, 33tl, 35t, 47t, 47b, 48b, 49t, 58t. The following photographs were taken at Trevor Scott's garden: pp.33b, 45. The photograph on page 58b was taken at Christopher Lloyd's garden. All photographs were taken by Jonathan Buckley.

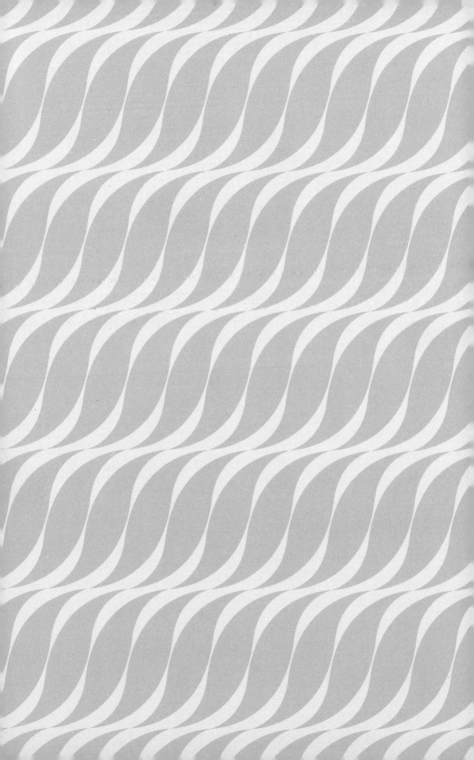